FOOD LOVERS

COOKIES

FOOD LOVERS

COOKIES

RECIPES SELECTED BY JONNIE LÉGER

Trans
Atlantic
Press

For best results when cooking the recipes in this book, buy fresh ingredients and follow the instructions carefully. Make sure that everything is properly cooked through before serving, and note that as a general rule vulnerable groups such as the very young, elderly people, pregnant women, convalescents and anyone suffering from an illness should avoid dishes that contain raw or lightly cooked eggs.

For all recipes, quantities are given in standard U.S. cups and imperial measures, followed by the metric equivalent. Follow one set or the other, but not a mixture of both because conversions may not be exact. Standard spoon and cup measurements are level and are based on the following:

1 tsp. = 5 ml, 1 tbsp. = 15 ml, 1 cup = 250 ml / 8 fl oz.

Note that Australian standard tablespoons are 20 ml, so Australian readers should use 3 tsp. in place of 1 tbsp. when measuring small quantities.

The electric oven temperatures in this book are given for conventional ovens with top and bottom heat. When using a fan oven, the temperature should be decreased by about 20–40°F / 10–20°C – check the oven manufacturer's instruction book for further guidance. The cooking times given should be used as an approximate guideline only.

CONTENTS

CHOCOLATE FLUSH COOKIES

Ingredients

7 oz / 200 g milk chocolate
(30% cocoa solids)

1/3 cup / 90 g unsalted butter

1/2 cup / 110 g superfine (caster) sugar

3 eggs

1 tsp vanilla extract

2 cups / 215 g all purpose (plain) flour

1/4 cup / 25 g cocoa powder

1/2 tsp baking powder

1 pinch salt

Method

Prep and cook time: 35 min plus 1 hr chilling time

1 Melt the chocolate and butter in a large pan over a low heat, stirring. Remove from the heat and stir in the sugar until dissolved.

2 Beat in the eggs, one at a time, followed by the vanilla.

3 Sift the flour, cocoa, baking powder and salt into a mixing bowl. Gradually stir in the chocolate mixture until combined. Cover the bowl and chill for 1 hour until firm.

4 Heat the oven to 325°F (160°C / Gas Mark 3). Line 2 large baking trays with non-stick baking paper.

5 Roll the chilled dough into 4 cm / 1½ inch balls and place well apart on the baking trays. Bake for 10–15 minutes until firm to the touch and the tops are cracked. Cool on the baking trays for a few minutes, then place on a wire rack to cool completely.

LEMON COOKIES

Ingredients

For the cookies:

1 cup plus 2 tbsp / 250 g butter

¾ cup / 150 g sugar

2½ cups / 250 g all purpose (plain) flour

1 cup / 125 g rice flour

For the glaze:

2½ cups / 250 g confectioners' (icing) sugar

1 lemon, juice and grated zest

Method

Prep and cook time: 35 min plus 30 min chilling time

1 Beat the butter and sugar in a mixing bowl until soft and light.

2 Sift in the flour and rice flour and mix to a smooth dough. Form into a ball, wrap in cling film (plastic wrap) and chill for 30 minutes.

3 Heat the oven to 350°F (180°C / Gas Mark 4). Line 2 large baking trays with non-stick baking paper.

4 Roll out the dough on floured surface about ¼ inch / 4 mm thick and cut out rounds about 1½ inches / 4 cm in diameter. Place on the baking trays.

5 Bake for 10–15 minutes until just golden. Cool on the baking trays for a few minutes, then place on a wire rack to cool completely.

6 For the glaze: sift the confectioners' (icing) sugar into a bowl and stir in enough lemon juice to give a coating consistency. Spread over the cookies and sprinkle with lemon zest. Leave to set.

WALNUT COOKIES

Ingredients

²/₃ cup / 150 g butter

½ cup / 110 g superfine (caster) sugar

1 egg yolk

1 tsp vanilla extract

¾ cup / 110 g very finely chopped walnuts

1¾ cups / 175 g all purpose (plain) flour

40 walnut halves

Method

Prep and cook time: 40 min plus 2 hrs chilling time

1 Beat the butter and sugar in a mixing bowl until soft and creamy.

2 Beat in the egg yolk, vanilla, walnuts and flour until combined. Wrap in cling film (plastic wrap) and chill for 2 hours.

3 Heat the oven to 325°F (160°C / Gas Mark 3). Line 2 large baking trays with non-stick baking paper.

4 Roll small pieces of the dough into 40 small balls. Place apart on the baking tray. Press a walnut half onto each ball.

5 Bake for 20 minutes until golden. Cool on the baking trays.

ROSEHIP AND ALMOND COOKIES

Ingredients

For the cookies:

1 cup / 225 g butter

¾ cup / 150 g sugar

2 eggs

4 tbsp milk

1½ tsp rosewater

1 cup / 110 g all purpose (plain) flour

½ tsp baking soda (bicarbonate of soda)

1 pinch salt

2 cups / 175 g rolled oats

1 cup / 75 g finely chopped almonds

To decorate:

1¾ cups / 200 g confectioners' (icing) sugar

4–6 tbsp rosehip syrup or cordial

Method

Prep and cook time: 30 min

1 Heat the oven to 400°F (200°C / Gas Mark 6). Line 2 large baking trays with non-stick baking paper.

2 Beat the butter and sugar in a mixing bowl until soft and light.

3 Beat in the eggs, milk and rosewater.

4 Sift in the flour and baking soda (bicarbonate of soda) and stir into the mixture with the salt, oats and almonds.

5 Drop spoonfuls of the mixture, apart, onto the baking trays and flatten with a fork. Bake for 8–10 minutes until golden. Cool on the baking trays for a few minutes, then place on a wire rack to cool completely.

6 For the icing: sift the confectioners' (icing) sugar into a bowl and stir in enough rosehip syrup or cordial to give a coating consistency. Spread over the cookies and leave to set.

CHOCOLATE NUT BALLS

Ingredients

For the cookies:

1¼ cups / 150 g all purpose (plain) flour

¾ cup / 100 g ground almonds

3 tbsp cocoa powder

scant ½ cup / 80 g sugar

½ cup / 125 g chilled butter, diced

1 egg, beaten

To decorate:

3–4 oz / 100 g dark (plain) chocolate

chopped pistachios

Method

Prep and cook time: 35 min plus 1 hr chilling time

1 Put the flour, almonds, cocoa powder and sugar into a mixing bowl. Rub in the butter until incorporated.

2 Stir in the egg and mix to a dough. Form into small balls, place on a plate, cover with cling film (plastic wrap) and chill for 1 hour.

3 Heat the oven to 350°F (180°C / Gas Mark 4). Line 2 large baking trays with non-stick baking paper.

4 Place the dough balls on the baking trays and bake for 10–12 minutes until firm. Cool on the baking trays for a few minutes, then place on a wire rack to cool completely.

5 To decorate: melt the chocolate in a heatproof bowl over a pan of simmering (not boiling) water. Remove from the heat. Dip the balls into the melted chocolate to half coat them and sprinkle with the pistachios. Place on a wire rack to set.

PIPED COOKIES WITH CHOCOLATE

Ingredients

½ cup / 110 g butter

3 tbsp confectioners' (icing) sugar

1 cup / 110 g all purpose (plain) flour

⅓ cup / 50 g ground hazelnuts

few drops vanilla extract

2½ oz / 75 g dark (plain) chocolate

Method
Prep and cook time: 40 min

1 Heat the oven to 350°F (180°C / Gas Mark 4). Line 2 large baking trays with non-stick baking paper.

2 Beat the butter and sugar in a mixing bowl until soft and creamy.

3 Stir in the flour, hazelnuts and vanilla until blended.

4 Spoon into a piping bag fitted with a large star-shaped nozzle and pipe 4 inch / 10 cm lines, well apart, on the baking trays.

5 Bake for 15–20 minutes until pale golden. Cool on the baking trays for a few minutes, then place on a wire rack to cool completely.

6 Melt the chocolate in a heatproof bowl over a pan of simmering (not boiling) water. Remove from the heat.

7 Dip one end of each cookie into the melted chocolate and place on a wire rack to set.

ICED HEARTS

Ingredients

For the cookies:

½ cup / 110 g unsalted butter

½ cup / 110 g superfine (caster) sugar

1 egg, lightly beaten

1 tsp vanilla extract

2¾ cups / 275 g all purpose (plain) flour

For the filling:

9 tbsp apricot jelly (jam)

1 tsp lemon juice

To decorate:

2½ cups / 250 g confectioners' (icing) sugar

2–3 tbsp water

A few drops pink food coloring

Method

Prep and cook time: 30 min

1 Heat the oven to 375°F (190°C / Gas Mark 5). Line a large baking tray with non-stick baking paper.

2 Beat the butter and sugar in a mixing bowl until soft and creamy. Gradually beat in the egg and vanilla.

3 Add the flour and mix to a dough.

4 Roll out the dough on a lightly floured surface to a thickness of ½ inch / 1 cm.

5 Using a heart-shaped cookie cutter, cut cookies out of the dough and place on the baking tray.

6 Bake for 8–10 minutes, until pale golden-brown. Cool on the baking tray for 5 minutes, then place on a wire rack to cool completely.

7 For the filling: put the jelly (jam) and lemon juice in a small pan and heat gently until melted. Bring to a boil and boil for 2–3 minutes. Set aside to cool and thicken.

8 For the icing: sift the confectioners' (icing) sugar into a bowl and stir in the water. Set one quarter of the icing aside. Color the remaining icing pink and spread over half the cookies.

9 Spread the jelly on the un-iced cookies and place an iced cookie on top. Drizzle with the reserved white icing and leave to set.

CHOCOLATE STICKS

Ingredients

For the cookies:

½ cup / 110 g butter

½ cup / 55 g confectioners' (icing) sugar

1¼ cups / 125 g all purpose (plain) flour

1 tbsp cocoa powder

To decorate:

3–4 oz / 100 g dark (plain) chocolate

Method

Prep and cook time: 45 min

1 Heat the oven to 350°F (180°C / Gas Mark 4). Line 2 large baking trays with non-stick baking paper.

2 Beat the butter and sugar in a mixing bowl until soft and creamy.

3 Sift in the flour and cocoa and gently stir until blended. Spoon into a piping bag fitted with a small nozzle and pipe 2½ inch / 6 cm lines, well apart, on the baking trays.

4 Bake for 15 minutes until firm. Cool on the baking trays for a few minutes, then place on a wire rack to cool completely.

5 To decorate: melt the chocolate in a heatproof bowl over a pan of simmering (not boiling) water. Remove from the heat. Dip one side of each cookie into the melted chocolate. Place on a wire rack to set.

ALMOND AND CHERRY COOKIES

Ingredients

¾ cup / 175 g unsalted butter

3 tbsp confectioners' (icing) sugar

½ tsp almond extract

1¾ / 175 g cups all purpose (plain) flour

3 tbsp cornstarch (cornflour)

6 candied (glacé) cherries, halved

Method

Prep and cook time: 30 min

1 Heat the oven to 350°F (180°C / Gas Mark 4). Line a large baking tray with non-stick baking paper.

2 Beat the butter and sugar in a mixing bowl until soft and creamy. Beat in the almond extract.

3 Sift in the flour and cornstarch (cornflour) and mix until blended.

4 Spoon into a piping bag fitted with a large star-shaped nozzle and pipe 12 stars onto the baking tray. Place a cherry half on top of each, pressing in lightly.

5 Bake for about 12 minutes, until pale golden. Cool on the baking trays for a few minutes, then place on a wire rack to cool completely.

ESPRESSO COOKIES

Ingredients

For the cookies:

¼ cup / 25 g espresso coffee beans

3 egg whites

¾ cup / 175 g superfine (caster) sugar

6 tbsp grated dark (plain) chocolate, (60% cocoa solids)

For the caramel cream:

⅔ cup / 130 g sugar

¾ cup / 180 ml light corn syrup (golden syrup)

1 cup / 240 ml whipping cream

4 tbsp butter

1 tsp vanilla extract

Method

Prep and cook time: 3 hrs plus 15 min chilling time

1 Heat the oven to 350°F (180°C / Gas Mark 4).

2 Put the coffee beans on a baking tray and roast for 8 minutes. Allow to cool, then crush finely.

3 Whisk the egg whites and sugar in a heatproof bowl over a pan of simmering (not boiling) water until thick.

4 Remove from the heat and continue whisking until the meringue forms stiff peaks. Whisk in the coffee beans and 3 tbsp grated chocolate.

5 Reduce the oven temperature to 275°F (140°C / Gas Mark 1). Line a large baking tray with non-stick baking paper.

6 Pipe or spoon about 20 rounds of meringue onto the baking tray. Bake for 2–2½ hours until dry and crisp. Cool on the tray, then remove from the paper. Sprinkle with the remaining grated chocolate.

7 For the caramel cream: put the sugar, syrup, and half the cream in a pan. Bring to a boil over a medium heat, stirring with a wooden spoon.

8 When the mixture boils, slowly add the remaining cream, stirring constantly. Add the butter and continue cooking over a medium heat, stirring occasionally, until a little of the mixture dropped into cold water can be rolled into a soft ball between your finger and thumb (240°F / 115°C on a sugar thermometer).

9 Remove from the heat and stir in the vanilla. Allow to cool and then chill until thick enough to pipe.

10 Spoon the caramel cream into a piping bag and pipe a swirl on top of each cookie.

PEANUT COOKIES

Ingredients

½ cup / 120 g butter

¾ cup / 150 g brown sugar

1 egg, beaten

1½ cups / 150 g all purpose (plain) flour

1 tsp baking powder

½ tsp ground cinnamon

½ tsp grated nutmeg

Finely grated zest of 1 orange

⅓ cup / 40 g whole, unsalted peanuts

¾ cup / 100 g unsalted peanuts, roughly chopped

1 cup / 80 g oats

Method

Prep and cook time: 30 min

1 Heat the oven to 400°F (200°C / Gas Mark 6). Line a large baking tray with non-stick baking paper.

2 Beat the butter and sugar in a mixing bowl until creamy and then stir in the egg.

3 Mix the flour, baking powder, cinnamon, nutmeg and orange zest together and stir into the butter mixture. Stir in the whole peanuts, ½ cup / 60g of the chopped peanuts and the oats.

4 Take teaspoons of the mixture and shape into round balls. Place the balls on the baking tray, well apart, and sprinkle with the remaining peanuts.

5 Bake for 15 minutes until golden. Cool on the baking tray for 5 minutes then place on a wire rack to cool completely.

SABLÉS WITH PISTACHIOS

Ingredients

1 cup / 100 g all purpose (plain) flour

5 tbsp confectioners' (icing) sugar

1 pinch salt

$^{1}/_{3}$ cup / 85 g unsalted butter, diced

1 small egg yolk

5 tbsp chopped pistachio nuts

Method

Prep and cook time: 30 min plus 2 hrs chilling time

1 Mix together the flour, confectioners' (icing) sugar and salt in a bowl.

2 Rub in the butter until the mixture resembles fine breadcrumbs. Add the egg yolk and mix to a dough.

3 Knead in the chopped pistachios. Roll the dough into a log, approximately 1 inch / 3 cm in diameter. Wrap in cling film (plastic wrap) and chill for 2 hours.

4 Heat the oven to 325°F (160°C / Gas Mark 3). Line a large baking tray with non-stick baking paper.

5 Slice the dough into rounds and place on the baking tray. Bake for 15 minutes, until light golden. Cool on the baking trays for a few minutes, then place on a wire rack to cool completely.

CHERRY CHOCOLATE COOKIES

Ingredients

1 cup / 200 g unsalted butter

½ cup / 85 g light brown sugar

½ cup / 85 g caster sugar

1 egg, beaten

2 cups / 225 g self-rising flour

4 oz / 100 g dark (plain) chocolate, (60% cocoa solids), roughly chopped

½ cup / 85 g dried cherries

Method

Prep and cook time: 25 min

1 Heat the oven to 375°F (190°C / Gas Mark 5). Line 2 large baking trays with non-stick baking paper.

2 Beat the butter and both sugars in a mixing bowl until soft and light.

3 Stir in the remaining ingredients until well blended.

4 Spoon about 20 heaps of the mixure onto the baking trays, spacing them well apart.

5 Bake for 12–15 minutes until just golden. Cool on the baking trays for a few minutes, then place on a wire rack to cool completely.

LAVENDER COOKIES

Ingredients

1 tbsp dried edible lavender flowers

¾ cup / 180 g butter, melted

⅓ cup / 75 g superfine (caster) sugar

3 cups / 300 g all purpose (plain) flour

½ tsp baking powder

¼ cup / 50 g sugar

To decorate:

1 tbsp dried lavender flowers

Method

Prep and cook time: 30 min plus 1 hr chilling time

1 Crush the lavender flowers and stir into the melted butter.

2 Add the superfine (caster) sugar, flour and baking powder and mix to a smooth dough. Divide the dough into 2 equal portions and shape into 1 inch / 3 cm thick rolls.

3 Roll in the sugar. Wrap in cling film (plastic wrap) and chill for 1 hour.

4 Heat the oven to 350°F (180°C / Gas Mark 4). Line 2 large baking trays with non-stick baking paper.

5 Cut each dough roll into thin slices and place on the baking trays. Bake for about 15 minutes, until golden. Cool on the baking trays for a few minutes, then place on a wire rack to cool completely.

6 Sprinkle with lavender flowers to decorate.

FLORENTINES

Ingredients

2 tbsp / 25 g butter

1/3 cup / 75 g superfine (caster) sugar

2 tsp all purpose (plain) flour

3 tbsp heavy (double) cream

1/2 cup / 110 g chopped candied fruit, e.g. angelica, apricots and cherries

3/4 cup / 50 g slivered (flaked) almonds

2 1/2 oz / 75 g dark (plain) chocolate

Method

Prep and cook time: 25 min

1 Heat the oven to 350°F (180°C / Gas Mark 4). Line a 12 hole bun tin with non-stick baking paper.

2 Heat the butter and sugar in a pan until melted. Heat until the mixture becomes golden brown.

3 Remove from the heat and stir in the flour and cream.

4 Add the fruit and nuts and mix well.

5 Spoon the mixture into the tins and spread out with a teaspoon. Bake for 12–15 minutes until golden brown. Cool in the tins for 10–15 minutes to set completely, before peeling off the baking paper.

6 Melt the chocolate in a heatproof bowl over a pan of simmering (not boiling) water. Spread a little chocolate onto the flat side of each Florentine and run a fork through the chocolate to create a wavy pattern before it sets.

ALMOND AND ORANGE COOKIES

Ingredients

1 cup / 225 g unsalted butter

1 cup / 110 g confectioners' (icing) sugar

Finely grated zest of 1 orange

3 cups / 300 g all purpose (plain) flour

1 pinch salt

1$^1/_3$ cup / 110 g slivered (flaked) almonds

Method

Prep and cook time: 30 min

1 Heat the oven to 375°F (190°C / Gas Mark 5). Line 2 large baking trays with non-stick baking paper.

2 Beat the butter and sugar in a mixing bowl until soft and creamy. Beat in the orange zest

3 Gradually beat in the flour and salt until the mixture begins to form a dough. Knead lightly until smooth.

4 Divide the dough into 30 pieces and roll each piece into a ball. Place well apart on the baking trays and press each ball lightly to flatten slightly. Press a few flaked almonds into each cookie.

5 Bake for 10–15 minutes until light golden. Cool on the baking trays for a few minutes, then place on a wire rack to cool completely.

PUFFED RICE COOKIES

Ingredients

½ cup / 110 g butter

¾ cup / 150 g sugar

1 egg

1 tsp vanilla extract

1 cup / 110 g all purpose (plain) flour

½ cup / 40 g rolled oats

½ tsp baking powder

1 pinch salt

1 cup / 25 g puffed rice

1/3 cup / 55 g white chocolate chips

Method

Prep and cook time: 30 min

1 Heat the oven to 350°F (180°C / Gas Mark 4). Line 2 large baking trays with non-stick baking paper.

2 Beat the butter and sugar in a mixing bowl until soft and creamy. Beat in the egg and vanilla.

3 Stir in the remaining ingredients. Place tablespoons of the mixture, well apart, on the baking trays.

4 Bake for 12–15 minutes until the edges are crisp and lightly browned. Cool on the baking trays for a few minutes, then place on a wire rack to cool completely.

CHOCOLATE AND PISTACHIO COOKIES

Ingredients

For the cookies:

2 cups / 200 g all purpose (plain) flour

¾ cup / 125 g ground almonds

1 cup / 200 g butter

½ cup / 100 g sugar

1 pinch salt

1 egg yolk

2–3 tbsp cream

For the filling:

7 oz / 200 g chocolate hazelnut spread

2–3 tbsp ground pistachios

To decorate:

7 oz / 200 g dark (plain) chocolate, (60% cocoa solids), chopped

1 tbsp butter

ground pistachios

Method

Prep and cook time: 45 min plus 1 hr chilling time

1 Heat the oven to 350°F (180°C / Gas Mark 4). Line 3 large baking trays with non-stick baking paper.

2 Put the flour and ground almonds into a mixing bowl. Add the butter, sugar, salt, egg yolk and cream and quickly chop all the ingredients with a knife. Tip out onto a work surface and mix to a smooth dough. Wrap in cling film (plastic wrap) and chill for 1 hour.

3 Roll out the dough on a lightly floured work surface to a thickness of ⅛ inch / 3 mm and cut out about 100 circles approximately 1¼ inches / 3 cm in diameter.

4 Place on the baking trays spaced apart and bake for about 12 minutes, until the cookies are lightly browned. Cool on the baking trays for a few minutes, then place on a wire rack to cool completely.

5 For the filling: mix the chocolate hazelnut spread with the ground pistachios and warm in a heatproof bowl over a pan of simmering (not boiling) water. Remove from the heat and cool until the mixture thickens. Sandwich the cookies together in pairs with the filling.

6 To decorate: melt the chocolate and butter in a heatproof bowl over a pan of simmering (not boiling) water. Dip one side of the sandwich cookies into the chocolate, allow the excess to drip off and place on a wire rack. Sprinkle at once with ground pistachios and leave to set.

WHITE CHOCOLATE COOKIES

Ingredients

1 cup / 225 g unsalted butter

1 cup / 225 g superfine (caster) sugar

½ tsp vanilla extract

¾ cup / 170 ml condensed milk

3½ cups / 350 g self-rising flour

5 oz / 150 g white chocolate, roughly chopped

Method

Prep and cook time: 30 min

1 Heat the oven to 350°F (180°C / Gas Mark 4). Line 2 baking trays with non-stick baking paper.

2 Beat the butter and sugar in a mixing bowl until pale and then stir in the vanilla and condensed milk.

3 Sift in the flour and work to a soft dough with your hands. Mix in the chocolate.

4 Roll small pieces of dough into balls and place well apart on the baking trays. Flatten with your fingers.

5 Bake for 15–18 minutes, until golden brown at the edges, but still a little soft.

6 Cool on the baking trays for a few minutes, then place on a wire rack to cool completely.

CRANBERRY PINWHEELS

Ingredients

For the dough:

½ cup / 110 g butter

¾ cup / 150 g sugar

1 egg

1 tsp vanilla extract

1¾ cups / 175 g all purpose (plain) flour

¼ tsp baking powder

1 pinch salt

For the filling:

½ cup / 50 g cranberries

¾ cup / 50 g finely chopped almonds

1 tbsp finely grated orange zest

1 tsp ground cinnamon

3 tbsp light brown sugar

Method

Prep and cook time: 45 min plus 4 hrs chilling time

1 Beat the butter and sugar in a mixing bowl until soft and creamy. Beat in the egg and vanilla.

2 Stir in the flour, baking powder and salt and mix to a soft dough. Form into a ball, wrap in cling film (plastic wrap) and chill for 1 hour.

3 For the filling: mash the cranberries in a bowl and stir in the almonds, orange zest, cinnamon and brown sugar.

4 Roll out the dough on a lightly floured surface to a 10 inches / 25 cm square. Spread with the cranberry mixture, leaving a ½ inch / 2 cm margin around the edges.

5 Roll up tightly, like a jelly (Swiss) roll. Wrap in cling film and chill for at least 3 hours or overnight.

6 Heat the oven to 375°F (190°C / Gas Mark 5). Line a large baking tray with non-stick baking paper.

7 Cut the roll into ¼ inch / 6 mm slices and place on the baking tray. Bake for about 15 minutes, until lightly browned. Cool on the baking tray for a few minutes, then place on a wire rack to cool completely.

COOKIE POPSICLES

Ingredients

For the cookies:

¾ cup / 175 g butter

¾ cup / 175 g superfine (caster) sugar

1 egg, beaten

3½ cups / 350 g all purpose (plain) flour

2 tbsp cornstarch (cornflour)

10 flat popsicle (lollipop) sticks

To decorate:

1 cup / 110 g confectioners' (icing) sugar

1 tbsp hot water

A few drops pink food coloring

Method

Prep and cook time: 40 min plus 30 min chilling time

1 Heat the oven to 350°F (180°C / Gas Mark 4). Line 2 large baking trays with non-stick baking paper.

2 Beat the butter and sugar in a mixing bowl until very soft, light and fluffy. Gradually add the egg, beating continuously.

3 Sift in the flour and cornstarch (cornflour) and mix well to form a fairly firm dough.

4 Knead lightly, then roll out the dough thinly on a lightly floured surface. Cut into 20 rounds, using a 2½ inch / 6.5 cm plain cutter.

5 Carefully sandwich two rounds of dough with a popsicle (lollipop) stick in between. Using a palette knife, place the cookies onto the baking trays and chill for 30 minutes.

6 Bake for 15 minutes, until lightly browned. Cool on the baking trays for a few minutes, then place on a wire rack to cool completely.

7 For the icing: sift the confectioners' (icing) sugar into a bowl and stir in enough hot water until thick enough to coat the cookies. Put half the icing into a small bowl and add the pink food coloring.

8 Spread the white icing over the cookies. Pipe the pink icing over the top as desired.

NUT AND CHOCOLATE MACAROONS

Ingredients

For the macaroons:

4 egg whites

1 cup / 200 g light brown sugar

1 tsp lemon juice

1 cup / 150 g ground hazelnuts

¾ cup / 100 g ground almonds

To decorate:

chocolate hazelnut spread

40 hazelnut halves

Method

Prep and cook time: 45 min

1 Heat the oven to 325°F (160°C / Gas Mark 3). Line 2 large baking trays with non-stick baking paper.

2 Whisk the egg whites until very stiff. Gradually add the sugar and lemon juice, whisking all the time.

3 Fold in the ground nuts.

4 Spoon small heaps onto the baking trays and bake for 30–35 minutes until golden brown. Cool on the baking tray for a few minutes, then place on a wire rack to cool completely.

5 Spoon the spread on top of each macaroon and top with half a hazelnut.

LEMON AND RAISIN COOKIES

Ingredients

1½ cups / 150 g all purpose (plain) flour

½ tsp baking powder

1 pinch salt

½ cup / 110 g superfine (caster) sugar

½ cup / 110 g butter, softened

1 egg, beaten

Finely grated zest of 1 lemon

1 cup / 150 g raisins

Method

Prep and cook time: 25 min

1 Heat the oven to 375°F (190°C / Gas Mark 5). Line 2 large baking trays with non-stick baking paper.

2 Sift the flour, baking powder and salt into a mixing bowl.

3 Beat in the sugar, butter, egg and lemon zest until well blended. Stir in the raisins.

4 Drop spoonfuls of the mixture, well apart, on the baking trays. Bake for 15 minutes until golden. Cool on the baking trays for a few minutes, then place on a wire rack to cool completely.

NUT STARS

Ingredients

For the cookies:

2 cups / 200 g all purpose (plain) flour

¼ cup / 40 g ground almonds

¼ cup / 40 g ground hazelnuts

½ cup / 100 g superfine (caster) sugar

1 pinch salt

1 cup / 200 g butter, diced

¾ cup / 50 g chopped almonds

To decorate:

1 cup / 100 g confectioners' (icing) sugar

1–2 tbsp lemon juice

Sugar stars

Method

Prep and cook time: 25 min plus 1 hr chilling time

1 Mix the flour with the ground nuts, sugar and salt. Add the butter and knead to a dough.

2 Knead in the chopped almonds and form the dough into a ball. Wrap in cling film (plastic wrap) and chill for 1 hour.

3 Heat the oven to 400°F (200°C / Gas Mark 6). Line 2 large baking trays with non-stick baking paper.

4 Roll out the dough on a floured surface, $1/8$ inch / 4 mm thick and cut into star shapes using a small star-shaped cookie cutter.

5 Place on the baking trays and bake for about 12 minutes until golden. Cool on the baking trays for a few minutes, then place on a wire rack to cool completely.

6 For the icing: sift the confectioners' (icing) sugar into a bowl and gradually beat in enough lemon juice to form a thick coating consistency.

7 Spread the icing over the stars and sprinkle with the sugar stars. Leave to set.

HEART-SHAPED JELLY COOKIES

Ingredients

For the cookies:

1 cup / 225 g unsalted butter

½ cup / 100 g superfine (caster) sugar

2 cups / 200 g all purpose (plain) flour

¾ cup / 100 g ground almonds

½ cup / 150 g seedless raspberry jelly (jam)

To decorate:

2–3 tbsp seedless raspberry jelly (jam)

2 tsp boiling water

sugar sprinkles

Method

Prep and cook time: 30 min plus 1 hr chilling time

1 Beat the butter in a mixing bowl until soft. Add the sugar, flour and ground almonds and mix with your hands to form a dough.

2 Knead the dough lightly until smooth. Wrap in cling film (plastic wrap) and chill for 1 hour.

3 Heat the oven to 300°F (150°C / Gas Mark 2). Line 2 large baking trays with non-stick baking paper.

4 Roll out the dough on a lightly floured surface, about ¼ inch / 6mm thick. Cut into heart shapes using a heart-shaped cookie cutter and place on the baking trays.

5 Bake for about 20 minutes until lightly golden. Cool on the baking trays for a few minutes, then place on a wire rack to cool completely.

6 Sandwich the cookies together with the jelly (jam).

7 To decorate: heat the jelly with the hot water until melted. Brush over the top of each heart and sprinkle with the sugar sprinkles.

APRICOT COOKIES

Ingredients

1 cup / 200 g unsalted butter, diced

3 cups / 300 g all purpose (plain) flour

1 cup / 90 g confectioners' (icing) sugar

2 egg yolks

1 tsp vanilla extract

1 cup / 150 g dried ready to eat apricots, finely chopped

Method

Prep and cook time: 25 min plus 30 min chilling time

1 Put the butter and flour into a mixing bowl and rub the butter into the flour until the mixture resembles breadcrumbs.

2 Stir in the sugar, egg yolks, vanilla and apricots and mix to a soft dough. Form into a ball, wrap in cling film (plastic wrap) and chill for 30 minutes.

3 Heat the oven to 400°F (200°C / Gas Mark 6). Line 2 large baking trays with non-stick baking paper.

4 Roll out the dough on a lightly floured surface, about ¼ inch / 6mm thick. Cut into about 20 rounds with a cookie cutter and place on the baking trays.

5 Bake for 10–12 minutes until lightly golden. Cool on the baking trays for a few minutes, then place on a wire rack to cool completely.

CHERRY-CHOCOLATE COOKIES

Ingredients

1 cup / 200 g unsalted butter

¾ cup / 170 g superfine (caster) sugar

1 egg, beaten

2 cups / 225 g self-rising flour

3½ oz / 100 g white chocolate, roughly chopped

¹/₃ cup / 85 g candied (glacé) cherries, finely chopped

Cherry jelly (jam), to serve

Method

Prep and cook time: 25 min

1 Heat the oven to 375°F (190°C / Gas Mark 5). Line 2 large baking trays with non-stick baking paper.

2 Beat the butter and sugar in a mixing bowl until soft and light.

3 Stir in the remaining ingredients until well blended.

4 Spoon about 20 heaps of the mixture onto the baking trays, spacing them well apart.

5 Bake for 12–15 minutes until just golden. Cool on the baking trays for a few minutes, then place on a wire rack to cool completely.

6 Serve with a spoonful of cherry jelly (jam).

WHOOPIE PIES

2 cups / 200 g all purpose (plain) flour

1 pinch salt

½ tsp baking powder

½ tsp baking soda (bicarbonate of soda)

½ cup / 45 g cocoa powder

1 tsp instant coffee powder

3 tbsp / 50 ml hot black coffee

4 tbsp / 60 ml hot water

¾ cup / 175 g light brown sugar

⅓ cup / 75 ml sunflower oil

1 egg

1 tsp vanilla extract

4 tbsp / 55 ml plain yogurt

For the filling:

1⅓ cups / 200 g chopped milk chocolate

7 tbsp / 100 ml whipping cream

¼ cup / 55 g unsalted butter

For the topping:

2 cups / 200 g confectioners' (icing) sugar

3 tbsp cocoa powder

3–4 tbsp / 50–70 ml boiling water

To decorate:

colored chocolate beans

Method

Prep and cook time: 45 min plus chilling: 30 min

1 Heat the oven to 350°F (180°C / Gas Mark 4). Line 3 large baking trays with non-stick baking paper.

2 Sift together the flour, salt, baking powder and baking soda (bicarbonate of soda).

3 Mix together the cocoa and coffee powder in a mixing bowl, then whisk in the hot coffee and hot water until completely dissolved.

4 Stir together the sugar and oil until combined and then whisk into the cocoa mixture until well combined.

5 Whisk the egg, vanilla and yogurt into the cocoa mixture until smooth.

6 Gently fold the dry ingredients into the cocoa mixture, until blended.

7 Drop 2 tablespoons of the mixture at a time onto the baking trays, keeping them about 2 inches / 4 cm apart.

8 Bake for 10-15 minutes, until cooked through. Insert a skewer into the center – it should come out clean. Cool on the baking trays for a few minutes, then place on a wire rack to cool completely.

9 For the filling: place the chocolate, cream and butter in a heatproof bowl over a pan of simmering (not boiling) water. Stir until melted and smooth. Remove from the heat and set aside to cool until thickened. Chill for 30 minutes.

10 Pipe or spread the flat side of a cold cake with a generous amount of filling. Place another half, flat side down, on top of the filling then press both halves together lightly.

11 For the topping: sift the confectioners' (icing) sugar and cocoa powder into a bowl. Gradually beat in enough boiling water to give a thick coating consistency. Spoon on top of the whoopie pies, spread with a palette knife and decorate with chocolate beans. Leave to set.

RAISIN COOKIES

Ingredients

1 cup / 220 g butter

1 cup / 200 g light brown sugar

½ cup / 100 g superfine (caster) sugar

1 tsp vanilla extract

2 eggs

2 cups / 200 g all purpose (plain) flour

1 tsp baking soda (bicarbonate of soda)

1 tsp ground cinnamon

1 pinch salt

3 cups / 250 g rolled oats

1 cup / 150 g raisins

Method

Prep and cook time: 35 min

1 Heat the oven to 350°F (180°C / Gas Mark 4). Line 2 large baking trays with non-stick baking paper.

2 Beat together the butter, brown sugar, caster sugar and vanilla in a mixing bowl until smooth. Beat in the eggs until blended.

3 Sift in the flour, baking soda (bicarbonate of soda), cinnamon and salt and mix well.

4 Stir in the oats and raisins until combined.

5 Place large heaped teaspoons of the mixture onto the baking trays, spacing them well apart.

6 Bake for 10–15 minutes until golden. Cool on the baking trays for 15 minutes, then place on a wire rack to cool completely.

SHORTBREAD STARS

Ingredients

For the cookies:

¹/₃ cup / 75 g unsalted butter

scant ¼ cup / 40 g superfine (caster) sugar

¾ cup / 75 g all purpose (plain) flour

¼ cup / 40 g rice flour

1 pinch salt

To decorate:

1 cup / 100 g confectioners' (icing) sugar

1–2 tbsp lemon juice

Method

Prep and cook time: 40 min

1 Heat the oven to 150°C (300°F / Gas Mark 2). Grease a large baking tray.

2 Beat the butter and sugar until soft and creamy.

3 Sift in the flour, rice flour and salt and mix with your hands to a smooth dough.

4 Roll out on a lightly floured surface and cut into star shapes using a small star-shaped cookie cutter.

5 Bake for 15–20 minutes until pale golden. Cool on the baking tray for a few minutes, then place on a wire rack to cool completely.

6 To decorate: sift the confectioners' (icing) sugar into a bowl and gradually beat in enough lemon juice to form a thick coating consistency.

7 Spread the icing over the stars and leave to set.

TRIPLE CHOCOLATE COOKIES

Ingredients

11 oz / 300 g dark (plain) chocolate (70% cocoa solids), cut into chunks

6 tbsp / 90 g butter

1 tsp vanilla extract

¾ cup / 150 g light brown sugar

1½ cups / 150 g self-rising flour

4 oz / 110 g milk chocolate (25% cocoa solids), cut into chunks

4 oz / 110 g white chocolate, cut into chunks

Method

Prep and cook time: 30 min

1 Heat the oven to 350°F (180°C / Gas Mark 4). Line 2 large baking trays with non-stick baking paper.

2 Put 3½ oz / 100 g dark (plain) chocolate into a large heatproof bowl over a pan of simmering (not boiling) water until melted. Remove from the heat and stir in the butter, vanilla and sugar.

3 Sift in the flour and stir gently until combined. Add the remaining plain chocolate chunks, milk chocolate chunks and half the white chocolate chunks and stir until combined.

4 Spoon heaps, spaced apart, onto the baking trays. Press the remaining white chocolate chunks into the top of each heap.

5 Bake for 10–12 minutes until starting to color. Cool on the baking trays.

MARSHMALLOW COOKIES

Ingredients

For the cookies:

1 cup / 200 g unsalted butter, diced

3 cups / 300 g all purpose (plain) flour

1 cup / 90 g confectioners' (icing) sugar

2 egg yolks

1 tsp vanilla extract

1 tbsp superfine (caster) sugar

For the filling:

10 white marshmallows

To decorate:

½ cup / 55 g confectioners' (icing) sugar

1–2 tsp hot water

Method

Prep and cook time: 30 min plus 30 min chilling time

1 Put the butter and flour into a food processor and blend until the mixture resembles breadcrumbs. Alternatively rub the butter into the flour in a mixing bowl.

2 Stir in the sugar, egg yolks and vanilla and mix to a soft dough. Form into a ball, wrap in cling film (plastic wrap) and chill for 30 minutes.

3 Heat the oven to 400°F (200°C / Gas Mark 6). Line 2 large baking trays with non-stick baking paper.

4 Roll out the dough on a lightly floured surface, about ¼ inch / 5mm thick. Cut into 20 squares and place on the baking trays. Sprinkle with caster sugar.

5 Bake for 10 minutes until lightly golden. Place a marshmallow on 10 cookies and return to the oven for 1–2 minutes until the marshmallows have melted. Place a plain cookie on top of each marshmallow cookie.

6 Cool on the baking trays for a few minutes, then place on a wire rack to cool completely.

7 To decorate: sift the confectioners' (icing) sugar into a bowl and add hot water to form a smooth icing. Drizzle over the top of each sandwiched cookie and leave to set.

PEANUT KISSES

Ingredients

½ cup / 110 g unsalted butter

½ cup / 125 g smooth peanut butter

½ cup / 110 g sugar

1 egg

2 tbsp milk

½ tsp vanilla extract

1¾ cups / 175 g all purpose (plain) flour

½ tsp salt

30 milk chocolate kisses

Method

Prep and cook time: 25 min plus 1 hr chilling time

1 Beat together the butter and peanut butter in a mixing bowl until creamy.

2 Beat in the sugar, egg, milk and vanilla. Stir in the flour and mix to a soft dough. Form into a ball and wrap in cling film (plastic wrap). Chill for 1 hour.

3 Heat the oven to 350°F (180°C / Gas Mark 4). Line 2 large baking trays with non-stick baking paper.

4 Shape the dough into 1 inch / 2.5 cm balls and place well apart on the baking trays. Gently flatten the balls and make a deep indentation in the center of each ball with a wooden spoon handle dipped in flour.

5 Bake for about 12 minutes, until golden. Immediately place a chocolate kiss into the center of each cookie. Place on a wire rack to cool completely.

CHOCOLATE CHUNK BARS

Ingredients

1 cup / 110 g self-rising flour

2 tbsp all purpose (plain) flour

1½ cup / 40 g desiccated coconut

½ cup / 100 g sugar

½ cup / 125 g butter, melted

14 oz / 400 g tin condensed milk

5 oz / 150 g dark (plain) chocolate (60% cocoa solids), cut into small chunks

3½ oz / 100 g milk chocolate (30% cocoa solids), cut into small chunks

3½ oz / 100 g white chocolate, cut into small chunks

Method

Prep and cook time: 45 min

1 Heat the oven to 350°F (180°C / Gas Mark 4). Grease a 9 inch / 23 cm square tin and line the base with non-stick baking paper.

2 Mix together both flours, the coconut, sugar, melted butter and condensed milk until well combined.

3 Spread over the base of the tin and scatter over two-thirds the dark (plain) chocolate and all the milk and white chocolate chunks.

4 Bake for 25–30 minutes until the top is firm. Immediately, lightly press the remaining dark chocolate chunks into the surface. Leave in the tin to become cold. Cut into squares or triangles to serve.

CHRISTMAS COOKIES

Ingredients

½ cup / 130 g butter

½ cup / 110 g superfine (caster) sugar

¼ teaspoon vanilla extract

1 large egg

2 tbsp cornstarch (cornflour)

3 tbsp self-rising flour

1½ cups / 150 g all purpose (plain) flour

⅓ cup / 110 g jelly (jam)

Method

Prep and cook time: 45 min plus 30 min chilling time

1 Heat the oven to 375°F (190°C / Gas Mark 5). Line 2 baking trays with non-stick baking paper.

2 Beat the butter and sugar in a mixing bowl until soft and light. Beat in the vanilla and egg.

3 Sift in the cornstarch (cornflour) and both flours and stir until combined. Chill for 30 minutes.

4 Roll heaped teaspoons of the mixture into balls and place on the baking trays. Make a deep indentation in the center of each ball with a wooden spoon handle dipped in flour.

5 Fill each indentation with ½ teaspoon of jelly (jam).

6 Bake for about 20 minutes, until pale golden. Cool on the baking trays for a few minutes, then place on a wire rack to cool completely.

CHOCOLATE CHIP COOKIES

Ingredients

½ cup / 125 g unsalted butter

scant ½ cup / 90 g superfine (caster) sugar

1 egg

1 egg yolk

1 tsp vanilla extract

1¾ cups / 175 g self-rising flour

3 oz / 90 g dark (plain) chocolate, chopped into small chunks

Method

Prep and cook time: 30 min

1 Heat the oven to 350°F (180°C / Gas Mark 4). Line 2 large baking trays with non-stick baking paper.

2 Beat the butter and sugar in a mixing bowl until soft and creamy.

3 Add the egg, yolk, vanilla and flour and stir well until blended.

4 Place small heaps of the mixture onto the baking trays, spacing them slightly apart to allow them to spread. Press the chocolate chunks onto the heaps and push down gently.

5 Bake for 10–15 minutes until golden. Cool on the baking trays for a few minutes, then place on a wire rack to cool completely.

LADY FINGERS

Ingredients

4 eggs, separated

½ cup / 110 g superfine (caster) sugar

¾ cup / 90 g all purpose (plain) flour

1 pinch salt

icing (confectioners') sugar

Method

Prep and cook time: 45 min

1 Heat the oven to 300°F (150°C / Gas Mark 2). Grease 2 large baking trays.

2 Whisk the egg yolks and half the sugar in a mixing bowl with an electric whisk until thick and mousse-like.

3 In another bowl whisk the egg whites until firmly peaking. Whisk in the remaining sugar and continue whisking until stiff.

4 Sift the flour and salt into the egg yolk mixture and gently fold in until incorporated.

5 Fold in the egg whites, a third at a time, until incorporated.

6 Spoon the mixture into a piping bag with a large plain nozzle. Pipe 4 inch / 10 cm lines on the baking trays and sift over a layer of confectioners' (icing) sugar.

7 Bake for 20 minutes until the tops have formed a crust. Cool on the baking trays for a few minutes, then place on a wire rack to cool completely.

8 Sift some confectioners' (icing) sugar over the fingers before serving.

COOKIES WITH CREAM AND BERRIES

Ingredients

For the cookies:

1 cup / 225 g unsalted butter

½ cup / 110 g superfine (caster) sugar

1 tsp vanilla extract

2¼ cups / 225 g all purpose (plain) flour

For the filling:

2 cups / 500 ml heavy (double) cream

2 tbsp confectioners' (icing) sugar

2 cups / 250 g raspberries

2 cups / 250 g blueberries

Method

Prep and cook time: 35 min plus 30 min chilling time

1 Beat the butter, sugar and vanilla in a mixing bowl until light and fluffy.

2 Sift in the flour and mix to a dough. Knead on a lightly floured surface until smooth. Wrap in cling film (plastic wrap) and chill for 30 minutes.

3 Heat the oven to 350°F (180°C / Gas Mark 4). Line 2 large baking trays with non-stick baking paper.

4 Roll out the dough on a lightly floured surface. Cut into 24 daisy shapes using a flower-shaped cookie cutter and place on the baking trays.

5 Bake for about 15 minutes until lightly golden. Cool on the baking trays for a few minutes, then place on a wire rack to cool completely.

6 For the filling: whisk the cream and confectioners' (icing) sugar until thick. Sandwich the cookies together in threes with the cream and berries, finishing with a topping of cream and berries. Serve immediately.

MEXICAN WEDDING COOKIES

Ingredients

1 cup / 225 g unsalted butter

1½ cups / 175 g confectioners' (icing) sugar

½ tsp vanilla extract

½ tsp almond extract

3 cups / 300 g all purpose (plain) flour

1 pinch salt

1¼ cups / 150 g chopped almonds

Method

Prep and cook time: 30 min

1 Heat the oven to 375°F (190°C / Gas Mark 5). Line 2 large baking trays with non-stick baking paper.

2 Beat the butter and 1 cup / 110 g confectioners' (icing) sugar in a mixing bowl until soft and creamy. Beat in the vanilla and almond extracts.

3 Gradually beat in the flour and salt until the mixture begins to form a dough. Add the almonds and knead lightly until combined.

4 Divide the dough into 30 pieces and roll each piece into a ball. Place well apart on the baking trays and press each ball lightly to flatten slightly.

5 Bake for 10–15 minutes until light golden. Cool on the baking trays for a few minutes, then place on a wire rack to cool completely.

6 Put the remaining confectioners' (icing) sugar into a bowl and add a few cookies at a time, shaking them gently until coated.

MACAROONS
WITH CHOCOLATE COFFEE CREAM

Ingredients

For the macaroons:

2 cups / 200 g ground almonds

½ cup / 100 g sugar

2 egg whites

confectioners' (icing) sugar

For the filling:

3½ oz / 100 g dark (plain) chocolate (70% cocoa solids), finely chopped

10 tsp / 50 ml whipping cream

1 tsp instant coffee powder

Method

Prep and cook time: 40 min

1 Heat the oven to 300°F (150°C / Gas Mark 2). Line a large baking tray with non-stick baking paper.

2 Mix the almonds with half the sugar.

3 Whisk the egg whites with the remaining sugar until very stiff and glossy.

4 Carefully fold the almond mixture into the egg whites and spoon into a piping bag with a plain nozzle.

5 Pipe 40–45 small heaps of the mixture (about ½ inch / 1 cm) onto the baking tray. Dust with confectioners' (icing) sugar and bake for 15 minutes. Switch off the oven and let the macaroons cool in the oven.

6 For the filling: melt the chocolate in a heatproof bowl over a pan of simmering (not boiling) water. Remove from the heat and allow to cool.

7 Warm the cream slightly and dissolve the instant coffee in it. Allow to cool and then whisk until stiff.

8 Fold the coffee cream into the cold melted chocolate.

9 Spread the chocolate filling onto half of the macaroons, top with the remaining macaroons, press lightly and serve dusted with confectioners' (icing) sugar.

CHOCOLATE BEAN COOKIES

Ingredients

½ cup / 110 g unsalted butter

½ cup / 110 g light brown sugar

1 egg, beaten

¾ cup / 75 g all purpose (plain) flour

¼ cup / 25 g cocoa powder

½ tsp baking soda (bicarbonate of soda)

scant 1½ cups / 110 g rolled oats

3 oz / 80 g colored chocolate beans

Method

Prep and cook time: 25 min

1 Heat the oven to 350°F (180°C / Gas Mark 4). Line 2 large baking trays with non-stick baking paper.

2 Beat the butter and sugar in a mixing bowl until soft and creamy.

3 Add the egg, flour, cocoa powder, baking soda (bicarbonate of soda) and oats and mix well.

4 Roll spoonfuls of the mixture into balls and place well apart on the baking trays. Flatten slightly and press a few chocolate beans into the top of each cookie.

5 Bake for 10–12 minutes until cooked through. Cool on the baking trays for a few minutes, then place on a wire rack to cool completely.

FLOWER COOKIES

Ingredients

1¾ cups / 175 g all purpose (plain) flour

½ tsp baking soda (bicarbonate of soda)

¹/₃ cup / 75 g unsalted butter

¹/₃ cup / 75 g superfine (caster) sugar

2 tbsp light corn syrup (golden syrup)

1 egg yolk

5 oz / 150 g red hard candy (clear boiled sweets), crushed

12–14 popsicle (lollipop) sticks or wooden skewers

Method

Prep and cook time: 25 min plus 30 min chilling time

1 Put the flour and baking soda (bicarbonate of soda) into a mixing bowl and rub in the butter until the mixture resembles breadcrumbs.

2 Add the sugar, syrup and egg yolk and mix to a dough. Form into a ball and wrap in cling film (plastic wrap). Chill for 30 minutes.

3 Heat the oven to 350°F (180°C / Gas Mark 4). Line a large baking tray with non-stick baking paper.

4 Roll out the dough thinly on a lightly floured surface. Cut into flower shapes using a flower-shaped cookie cutter. Using a small round cutter, cut out the center of each 'flower'. Place on the baking tray. Press a popsicle (lollipop) stick into each cookie.

5 Bake for 5 minutes. Put the crushed candies (sweets) into the center of each cookie and bake for a further 5 minutes, until the candies have melted and spread to fill the centers. Cool on the baking tray until the melted sweets have hardened.

ITALIAN PINE NUT COOKIES

Ingredients

2–3 cups / 200–300 g pine nuts

1½ cups / 140 g confectioners' (icing) sugar

6 oz / 160 g marzipan, chopped

finely grated zest of 1 lemon

2 egg whites

1¼ cups / 130 g self-rising flour

Method

Prep and cook time: 30 min

1 Heat the oven to 350°F (180°C / Gas Mark 4). Line 2 large baking trays with non-stick baking paper.

2 Put 1 cup / 100 g pine nuts, the sugar and marzipan into a food processor and process until crumbly.

3 Add the lemon zest and egg whites and pulse until combined. Add the flour and pulse until combined.

4 Roll the dough into 1 inch / 2 cm balls and roll each in the whole pine nuts, pressing the nuts on. Place apart on the baking trays and flatten slightly. Bake for 20 minutes, until lightly browned. Cool on the baking trays for a few minutes, then place on a wire rack to cool completely.

GINGER COOKIES

Ingredients

1½ cups / 150 g all purpose (plain) flour

½ tsp baking soda (bicarbonate of soda)

1 tsp ground ginger

1 pinch ground cinnamon

1 pinch ground cloves

¼ cup / 55 g butter

½ cup / 110 g superfine (caster) sugar

1 small egg, beaten

2 tbsp molasses (black treacle)

½ tsp lemon juice

⅓ cup / 75 g coarse sugar crystals

Method

Prep and cook time: 25 min

1 Heat the oven to 325°F (160°C / Gas Mark 3). Line 2 large baking trays with non-stick baking paper.

2 Sift the flour, baking soda (bicarbonate of soda) and spices into a bowl. Set aside.

3 Beat the butter and sugar in a mixing bowl until soft and creamy. Beat in the egg.

4 Stir in the molasses (treacle) and lemon juice, then stir in the flour mixture to form a soft dough.

5 Roll the dough into 1 inch / 2 cm balls and roll in the sugar crystals to coat. Place well apart on the baking trays.

6 Bake for about 12 minutes until firm and golden. Cool on the baking trays for a few minutes, then place on a wire rack to cool completely.

PISTACHIO AND ALMOND COOKIES

Ingredients

¾ cup / 175 g unsalted butter

½ cup / 90 g superfine (caster) sugar

1 egg, beaten

1¾ cups / 200 g self-rising flour

½ cup / 90 g finely chopped candied peel

¾ cup / 75 g chopped pistachio nuts

¾ cup / 50 g chopped almonds

Method

Prep and cook time: 25 min

1 Heat the oven to 350°F (180°C / Gas Mark 4). Line 2 large baking trays with non-stick baking paper.

2 Beat the butter and sugar in a mixing bowl until soft and creamy, then beat in the egg.

3 Gently stir in the flour until incorporated. Stir in the candied peel and nuts.

4 Drop spoonfuls of the mixture, slightly apart, onto the baking trays and bake for 12–15 minutes until golden. Cool on the baking trays for a few minutes, then place on a wire rack to cool completely.

Published by Transatlantic Press

First published in 2012

Transatlantic Press
38 Copthorne Road, Croxley Green, Hertfordshire WD3 4AQ

© Transatlantic Press

Images and Recipes by StockFood © The Food Image Agency

Recipes selected by Jonnie Léger, StockFood

A catalogue record for this book is available from the British Library.

ISBN: 978-1-907176-87-6

Printed in China